D1742359

Other books written by Christine Shannon:

A Children's Book: "Mickey and Hip Hop"

About a boy and his pet frog.

A Mother's Love Forever

*"Spiritual Phenomena
Based on True Facts"*

CHRISTINE M. SHANNON

BALBOA.
PRESS
A DIVISION OF HAY HOUSE

Copyright © 2018 Christine M. Shannon.

All rights reserved. No part of this book may be used or reproduced by any means, graphic, electronic, or mechanical, including photocopying, recording, taping or by any information storage retrieval system without the written permission of the author except in the case of brief quotations embodied in critical articles and reviews.

Balboa Press books may be ordered through booksellers or by contacting:

Balboa Press
A Division of Hay House
1663 Liberty Drive
Bloomington, IN 47403
www.balboapress.com
1 (877) 407-4847

Because of the dynamic nature of the Internet, any web addresses or links contained in this book may have changed since publication and may no longer be valid. The views expressed in this work are solely those of the author and do not necessarily reflect the views of the publisher, and the publisher hereby disclaims any responsibility for them.

The author of this book does not dispense medical advice or prescribe the use of any technique as a form of treatment for physical, emotional, or medical problems without the advice of a physician, either directly or indirectly. The intent of the author is only to offer information of a general nature to help you in your quest for emotional and spiritual well-being. In the event you use any of the information in this book for yourself, which is your constitutional right, the author and the publisher assume no responsibility for your actions.

Any people depicted in stock imagery provided by Thinkstock are models, and such images are being used for illustrative purposes only.
Certain stock imagery © Thinkstock.

Print information available on the last page.

ISBN: 978-1-5043-9602-8 (sc)
ISBN: 978-1-5043-9604-2 (hc)
ISBN: 978-1-5043-9603-5 (e)

Library of Congress Control Number: 2018900986

Balboa Press rev. date: 01/31/2018

Contents

"The spiritual phenomenon in this book are based on true facts."

Dedication

I dedicate this book to my dear Mother who is always in my heart with perpetual love and gratitude. Till we meet again Mom.

Acknowledgments

With many thanks to all my doctors and medical team for their support, kindness and understanding. Their dedication and care was of high caliber.

1

Divergence

As life moves on, we learn it's filled with ups and downs. It can be so unpredictable, too, don't you think? One minute you're riding high, and the next minute, the rug is pulled out from under you. But we know to get up, dust ourselves off, try to make it better, and go with what may come. That's what I did after giving my two-week notice and leaving the banking industry. I never looked back. I used to look forward to getting up and going to work, but after repeated mergers, the downsizing of employees, and restructuring, well, let's just say I had my fill, and it was now overflowing. So I said goodbye and retired in December 2004, after nineteen years of devoted service.

After being home and getting things done that were left on the back burner, I decided to get a job. Now was my chance to do something different. Going on job interviews after nineteen years was not the easiest thing for me. I thought bringing all my achievement awards to the interviews would show I was capable. I hoped it would help me land a job. Wrong! The interviews went really well, but I was told I was overqualified. So I gave the interviews a rest and went to a bookstore to purchase a book on what to say and do at job interviews. My God, what happened to just being yourself? It had some good points, I must admit, but most of it was just ridiculous to me.

I like people and decided to do something with some fun in it. I applied to and was hired at a large, commercial, craft store chain. The store was just built and was nothing but a huge, empty shell when I applied. I and others helped build the inside, setting up shelves and putting up stock. It was something that I had never done, and I absolutely loved it. It had some challenges involved, for sure.

After the store was completed, I was trained for a cashier position. Plus, I was taught many crafts, such as using knitting looms to make hats and scarfs and how to make flower arrangements and wreaths with silk flowers. Yes, things were looking pretty good. I was happy again. I performed demonstrations for customers, showing how the knitting looms where used. I made blankets for my family members and hats and scarfs for friends. The pay was small, but the rewards were great in working with such nice people and learning an abundance of crafts. I loved my retirement and my new job. But then things started to spiral slowly downward after working at my new, fun job from March 2006 until May 2007.

2

The Cottage

Every summer, my husband and I go to northern Michigan on vacation to our summer cottage, which was passed down to me from my mother and father. While there, we do many things. For instance, we walk a mile after breakfast every morning. After our walk, we drive into town. It being a good thirty-minute drive, we enjoy the view on the way of dense forests, green lush fields and hills. Sometimes we get a glimpse of deer and turkey's that are strolling on the side of the road. Oh, and bear too! Not too many of those, but we have seen a couple. That's okay with me. We visit the shops and a favorite bookstore I adore there. The rest of the day is spent just having good ole fun. We top the late afternoon and evening with a great dinner and relaxation sitting in the backyard overlooking the lake and watching for different birds, deer and just about anything else that will stroll by.

Of course, there is always work involved while we are there. My parents' dream was to finish the cottage, but they never had that chance. It was bought as a shell: a structure with a roof, walls, and foundation. Nothing else. No running water or electricity. My father installed a crayon red, old-fashioned hand pump in the backyard. When we needed water, we had to prime the pump moving the handle up and down, until the water from the ground came out of the spout. The water was crystal clear and very cold. And yes, the commode was outside, too, in a small metal shed that we called the outhouse. Going out to it at night was pretty scary. Not to mention the many mosquito bites you had by the time you got back into the cottage. I'll never forget it. I called it "roughing it" when we were going up there. Neither the pump nor the outhouse are there anymore, thank goodness. The trusty red pump was taken out and now sits in a box. I just can't get rid of it; you just never know when it may be needed again. A lot of hard work went into the cottage to achieve some of the needed necessities at that time. We were just glad we had water. I sure learned some survival tips from the experience. When I went up with my parents, my father had me help feed the electrical wire in the walls, nail this, and drill that. Stuff like that. But I was glad to help. The cottage finally had running water, electricity, and heat. And yes, the commode was inside finally too. The walls were paneled and the floor tiled. The bedrooms were sectioned off from each other with doors.

The cottage has come a long way, but it's not quite completed yet. My husband, our son, and my goal is to finish it for my parents as they dreamed it to be. Every year, a little more gets done, and it won't be long now. We are really going to celebrate when that day comes.

There are so many fond memories. In the living room, on the wall above the sofa, hangs a picture of my mother and father that I took. Both are standing, very dressed up, and happily smiling the best smiles I had ever seen on them at the same time. I had the picture enlarged, framed, and put there to stay as a remembrance of the love they had for the cottage and our love for them. My father bought the cottage for my mother as a wedding anniversary present one year. What a surprise to her! She loved it so much.

Sadly, my mother passed away in 1997, and my father passed in 1998. Not even a year apart from each other. They were only sixty-five years of age when they died. So young yet. Just when they should have been enjoying their lives the most, their health declined. They were such brave fighters, battling their sicknesses till the end. I miss them both dearly.

After my mother passed, I would smell her perfume she always wore. It was called Wind Song. I often smelled it in my house. My father kept everything as was left in my mother's bedroom. It was my mother's wish to be cremated. After the funeral ceremony, he put her ashes in her room until his time would come, and then they would be together at their resting place. As the executor, I saw that their wishes were carried out, and they now rest peacefully together.

During this sad time, back at their house and not knowing where to begin, I walked around, just looking at all I was up against. I walked into my mother's room, and there on her dresser I noticed a perfume bottle. It was her perfume, Wind Song. I walked over and picked it up. There was some in it. I smelled the tip, where the perfume disburses from its container, and the thought of my mother nearby ran through me. It was the only thing I had now that brought me close to her. I took the bottle home with me I and put it on my bedroom dresser, where I would smell her fragrance and keep her close. After some years, I noticed one day that I didn't smell the fragrance. I picked up the bottle and tried to spray it, but none came out. I then smelled the tip, and the scent was very faint. It was empty. I felt sad and empty too.

3

A Visitor from Heaven

Every year when the weather starts to warm and the frost is gone, an eager feeling comes over me. It's like the cottage magnetizes me to come. Once I'm there, it gives me such inner peace, along with the fresh air and quiet, that puts me at ease with everything. There is a curved lake behind it. A marsh in the middle draws different birds, some that nest there, and deer come to drink from it. The tall grasses of the marsh dance in the wind in a synchronized, graceful fashion. Birds I've never seen before fly to trees farther away. My eyes look out over the beauty God put on this earth for us, and I wonder if other people really appreciate it as much as I do.

Sleeping is the best too. At night, you can hear a pin drop, it is so quiet and still. This leads me to tell you an event that took place there. It was different from any night I had ever known. As we got ready to go to bed one night, I opened our bedroom window partway. It was a beautiful, peaceful night, and a light breeze was coming through. Something had awakened me. I lay in bed with my eyes open for a moment. I was going to roll over on my side when I looked over at my husband, who was sound asleep. Just then, I heard it again. Something was coming from the bedroom window. It was like a light tapping sound. Our bedroom window wasn't your modern window that you unlock and pull up to open. Ours was like an old-fashioned shutter window. It was opened by a curved metal latch on the side, and when unlocked, it opened like a door, with a window screen exposed. The window was partly closed. The curtain blocked my view, so I couldn't see directly out. *Probably a critter of some sort, getting into something,* I thought. Eager to see what kind of critter it was, I leaned forward and placed my hand on the window frame.

I opened it slowly toward me so I could lean forward and look outside. Gazing out, I couldn't believe what I was looking at! I was totally enthralled. It was my mother! It was my mother's face aglow at the window. Her face appeared larger than normal and was close to the window screen. Maybe it just seemed that way to me because all I focused on was her face. She was smiling at me. I noticed her hand slowly motioning me to come with her. I don't recall seeing any other parts of her body. Just her smiling face and her hand in a slow, waving motion. Like they were the only things she wanted me to focus on. She looked well, not at all like she did when she was so ill. Her hair was all in place, just as it always had been. She even had her glasses on.

I wanted to go out and hug her so much, but something held me back. All I could do was stare at my mother who was deceased and my mind clouded with thoughts: is this really happening? I didn't speak, and neither did my mother. We had eye contact with each other, and something warm and calming came over me. I can't imagine the expression on my face. I could only look at her and slowly move my head in a no response. My mind was racing, and I thought, *I don't want to go. Where does she want to take me?* I looked beyond her and could only see in the distance the dark night and part of the lake from the twilight night sky. As I gazed back at her, her face slowly faded in the darkness. I have no concept of how long she was at the window. But after she left, I kept gazing outside in wonderment. The night was black and still, except for what was now a luminous sky full of stars that shed light to where I could see the curved lake behind the cottage.

It was truly a wondrous beautiful night. I wasn't afraid but astounded at what I had just seen. My mother. My dear mother, who passed away in 1997. It had been nine years! I couldn't believe she appeared to me. I gazed over at my husband, who was still asleep. I quietly closed the window most of the way and lay down with never a thought of waking him. He sleeps hard, and waking him would result in a groggy state of mind. And most likely, he would not remember clearly what I told him about what I just witnessed. I'd tell him in the morning. I thought, *Did I really see her? I am awake. I did see her. It was truly my mother.* She didn't speak. She just waved her hand to come and smiled. But why? I lay still next to my husband with what had taken place going over and over in my head until I finally fell asleep.

4

Augury

It was a beautiful morning. Blue skies and full of sunshine. I couldn't wait to tell my husband about what I had seen. I made a big breakfast, as I always did while we were there. While we ate, I said to him, "You're probably not going to believe this, but I have to tell you something really important about what I saw at the bedroom window last night." Taking a bite of his bacon, he listened, looking at me intently as I told him everything. I told him I wasn't dreaming, and I was fully awake. I was not afraid but surprised at what I was looking at. I thought it was an animal of some sort making noise outside that woke me. But it was my mother's face, smiling and waving her hand, wanting me to come with her.

He didn't say much. He seemed surprised to hear it was my mother and not a critter. I don't think he knew how to respond about what he heard. He said he didn't hear anything that night. We finished our breakfast, and after cleaning up, we got started with our day. All that day, I couldn't stop thinking and talking about it. That night, when we went to bed, I left the window closed, which resulted in no occurrence like the night before.

Unfortunately, after our wonderful few days at the cottage, it was time to go home and take care of things there, like cutting the grass. But we wouldn't be there long as we spent most of our summers going back and forth between our two places. Now, not long after returning home, I had a dream. I dreamed I was in a room of nicely dressed people. It was a loquacious atmosphere. I don't recall what the conversation was about, only that it was pleasant. Suddenly, I heard a soft tapping sound. Then it got louder. I turned in the direction of the tapping. It was coming from a window in the room I was in. There at the window was the face of my mother again, just smiling. Then I woke up. I told my husband about the dream I had that morning and said to him, "She is trying to tell me something. Why does she keep coming to me and persist in getting my attention?" My husband is a very conscientious listener and agreed with me. I had this same dream twice since we returned home from the cottage.

5

Message Received

My mother had a history of cancer. She underwent radiation treatments for colon cancer. I remember how sick she had gotten from it. She would come home after her treatment and lie down on the sofa. She was so weak. I remember her showing me her stomach that had been slightly burned from the intensity of the radiation. I felt so bad for her. She was an active person, and it was so hard to see her idle like that. I used to bring her cheery balloons after I got off work to try to get her to smile. She didn't smile much, but I think she was just glad I was there. Then the good news came. We were all so glad to hear she survived the cancer.

With her spiritually appearing to me at the window up north, and the dreams that followed, I started to think that maybe she was trying to warn me about my colon. I had never had a colonoscopy, and being in my fifties and with the family cancer history, I thought it was time to have one done. So I went to the doctor and was scheduled for a colonoscopy. I was thankful the test results came back fine. Nothing wrong there, thank God. So reflecting on my mother again, my thoughts were, *Maybe she's warning me of breast cancer.* For some reason, I just had a strong feeling that she was trying to convey something serious. I went to the doctor and was given a referral for a mammogram. Everything came back fine with that, too.

Now mind you, I wasn't having anymore dreams with my mom at this time. But something inside me told me that I must be on the right track with having these tests done. So I thought I should go and have a Pap test done. My last Pap smear test was done in December 2004, just before retiring from my job at the bank. It was now 2007. I had always kept up with yearly Pap tests. But I fell behind because time had lapsed on my insurance, time spent searching for a new job, and all. Thank goodness for the medical insurance package I had gotten through my new job, or I wouldn't have been able to get these tests done. Being a part-time employee, the insurance I had wasn't the best, but it was something I truly appreciated.

I finally was scheduled for an appointment and went to my primary physician to have a Pap test. I received the tests results, and there it was! There was the problem! The results came back abnormal. I was stunned by the news. Just to make sure, I had it done again by a different doctor for a second opinion, and again it came back with the same result: abnormal. Now I knew why my mother appeared to me at the window at the cottage and in my dreams. She came to warn me I had cancer. My eyes filled with tears. That night, all I could do was stare out the window and picture my mother's face. I was so amazed and felt my heart full of love and gratefulness. My husband was astonished as well that she appeared to warn me but upset about the test results. He said, "Don't worry, Chris. It will all be fine." I could tell he was worried and very concerned for me. He and my son were very supportive through it all. Anything I needed, they were both right there and so helpful. I don't know what I would have done without them. They are the best and the loves of my life.

6

Coping with Life's Obstacles

The second Pap test was done at a cancer institute and based in midtown Detroit. I had a scheduled consultation with my assigned doctor there about the tests results. I was told I was fifty-four years of age with high-grade SIL on pap and atypical glandular cells. I had surgery where I had a negative ECC, cervical biopsies, and inadequate colposcopy.

My husband and I had just purchased my father-in-law's motor home and had plans in the works to travel to Florida, visiting friends on the way and staying on the MacDill Air Force Base there. We decided to stick with our plans, take our trip for a few weeks, and get away from our Michigan home's cold weather for a while. But only a couple of days into our stay in Florida, I received a phone call from the cancer institute, asking if I could come in for a consultation regarding my tests results. A terrible feeling came over me. I explained we were in Florida, but an appointment was made, and we cut our vacation short and returned home.

I went to my scheduled appointment with my oncologist, when I was informed that I needed surgery. The procedure was scheduled.

On January 23, 2008, a procedure was performed, consisting of a cold knife conization of the cervix, endocervical curettage, a dilation and curettage of the uterine cavity, and a radical hysterectomy. Two of my lymph nodes were also removed. I was discharged from the hospital on January 25. My recovery took about six weeks. I could not drive or walk up steps; basically, I couldn't do anything. I really didn't feel like doing anything. I felt miserable.

7

Preparing for What's Ahead

After my recovery was complete, I saw my oncologist for a second consultation. My doctor informed me I had stage 2 cancer and requested that I undergo six weeks of chemotherapy and radiation which began on 3/20/08 consisting of five days a week of radiation with every Thursday adding chemotherapy as well as radiation.

Before my treatments began, however, an appointment was made for me to have a few things done. I went to my scheduled appointment at the cancer institute, where I was asked to lie on a table and was measured. An elongated plastic tub with a thick substance in it was brought in. I was told that a mold was going to be made from approximately the top back of both legs down to part of my calves. This would protect against any body movement during radiation treatments. I saw quite a few of them on shelves in the radiation room. They were all tagged with the owner's personal identification. When you came for your treatments, it was slid under you, and your legs rested in it perfectly. It was actually very comfortable.

After that, I was directed to a room where I had to put on a hospital gown and was told to lie on a gurney. I was told that four small, black, permanent ink dots were going to be placed on me. One would be on each side of my hip, one on my lower back, and one on my lower abdomen. These dots acted as a measuring tool for the radiation machine to locate the precise placement for where radiation would be applied. I will have these dots for the rest of my life.

8

Emotional Disarray

I felt so alone when I was diagnosed with cancer. I felt like my body was violated, and something terrible was happening beyond my control. You really can't explain to someone how you actually feel. There are no words to describe it. You go through so many emotions. I didn't share my feelings with too many people. I was bitter and upset, and I needed so many answers. I just didn't want to discuss it.

Having to have chemotherapy upset me the most. I considered myself healthy. I exercised, ate right, and was never one to sit still; I always had to be busy. But when I heard the word "chemo," that was the hardest for me. It meant that chemicals were going to be pumped into my bloodstream. I really had a hard time with that. My heart was so heavy with anger and sadness. I didn't know how to release it except to grab a pillow one day and scream and scream till I couldn't scream anymore. Then the tears came. I thought of my mother, and calmness then came over me. While trying to control my tears and wiping them away, I realized my mother had saved my life. I could feel her close, like she was beside me. *It could have been so much worse,* I thought while trying to calm myself. I was so thankful I had the tests done when I did. You see, there are no symptoms with cervical cancer, so it's very hard to detect unless a Pap test is done.

I had to be at the cancer institute at 7:30 a.m. on a Thursday for my first chemo appointment. I was told to go to the infusion room." I was so nervous and did not know what to expect. My husband and I walked down a long hall to the infusion room.

We approached a desk, and I was asked to sign in. I was then told to have a seat in the waiting area for my name to be called. We sat down and looked around. The infusion room was large. There were only four people already quietly sitting and waiting their turns. Televisions were mounted on the walls, and books and magazines were available on tables. When my name was called, I could see the strain on my husband's face. I gave him a reassuring smile and said, "I'll see you in a little while," and walked toward the nurse.

I was led through a big metal door to a room where they took a vial of blood, my vital signs, and weighed me. After that, I was told to go back and sit in the waiting area until my blood results came back. When my name was called again, a nice nurse led me through two large, metal, swinging doors and to a room with a bed, TV, and an IV monitor stand. The room had a glass wall that overlooked the hallway and other rooms like mine, with people in them hooked up to their IV monitor stands. My care management team was all so very nice and helpful. I loved my nurse, who had to prepare my IV. She was always so pleasant, caring, and gentle. My veins tend to want to move, and this nurse found one every time. She used a needle called a "butterfly" on me. I hardly felt a thing, just a little prick. I got into bed and was asked if I needed anything. I replied, "I'm so cold," and someone brought me a nice heated blanket. It felt so good. My nurse came back with a bag of liquid and put it on a hook located on the digital monitor stand. She asked me my name, birthdate, and personal identification number. Feeling her close, my thoughts were of my mother and that I had to do this. *This is going to help me get well,* I thought. I just wanted it to be all over with. I wished it was like before this had happened.

As the chemo flowed through my IV, I felt tears run down my cheeks. I turned to the TV and hoped it would take my mind to another place. It took approximately three hours before I was finished with my first chemo treatment. I was then led back to the infusion waiting area, where I rejoined my husband and was given directions on how to get to the radiation area for my first radiation therapy treatment. As I walked through the infusion room with my husband, I looked around, and now the whole waiting area was filled with people waiting their turns. Tears filled my eyes, but I wouldn't let them go any farther than that.

9

New Surroundings

Radiation was done in the basement area of the building. I would undergo treatments five days a week. To get to the area, we had to walk down long halls with no windows. Signs on the walls had arrows pointing in the direction to get there. Once there, we walked into a lobby, and I went to the desk to check in. I was then directed to go down another long hall to the waiting room. Off the waiting room was a changing room with lockers. There I would put on a hospital gown and go back into the waiting area and sit with the other patients for my name to be called. There were TVs mounted on the walls. Coffee and water were available, along with cookies and crackers.

I looked around the room. Everyone looked like one another: tired, no smiles, all dressed in hospital gowns, looking at magazines, or watching TV with few conversations going on. I felt alone and scared, but my husband would walk by the room, and our eyes would meet. He would give me a warm, reassuring smile as if to say, "I'm here, and it's going to be all right. Don't be afraid."

Every now and then I heard a bell. It reminded me of a cowbell. Every time I heard it, some people would applaud, and then I'd see smiles. While sitting and waiting for my name to be called, I asked a woman next to me what it was all about. She looked at me with a smile and warm eyes and said there was a bell in the hall across from the radiation room. "When it's your last day of treatment, you get to ring the bell to celebrate," she told me. Well, I was all for that. I couldn't wait for my last day. Everybody looked forward to it;

you could see it on their faces. It was nice to see smiling faces in the room when the bell was rung.

My name was called, and after what seemed a long wait, I was led to the radiation room for my first treatment. I didn't know what it was going to feel like; I just wanted to be at home. I was led to a table, and the nurse went to the shelf with the molds. She asked my name and personal identification, and mine was then brought to me and put on the table. I was asked to get on the table, lie on my back, and rest my legs in the mold. She positioned my hips to align with the markings on the table. She told me not to move and then covered me with a sheet from the waist down. She said it would not take long at all. All I could think to respond was, "Okay, thank you." I was so nervous.

She stepped behind a wall, and the radiation machine above me started to move to be adjusted and in line with the permanent spots I was given. All I remember from that point on was her saying, "You are finished. See, that didn't take long." She came to the table and removed my mold to be put back on the shelf for the next time. I didn't feel any pain or, in fact, anything while being radiated that day. That would unfortunately change as time with my treatments went on.

10

The Bell

I felt fatigued and was losing weight. My appetite was hardly there. I thought my last week of treatments would never come. Everything seemed to take so long. My doctor told me not to go out where there were many people because my resistance was so low, and I could contract just about any illness that was going around. I was so tired, all I wanted to do was sleep. The forty-five-minute drive every day was really getting me down.

One cold winter morning on the way to the cancer institute, my husband stopped at a stop sign just a short distance down our street, and a car hit us from behind. I was glad everybody was okay, but there was minor damage done to both cars. So with my nerves fringed, we still made it to my treatment appointment on time. That was a pretty bad day for the both of us.

The day of my last radiation treatment finally came! I would have forgotten it was my last day if the nurse hadn't mentioned it to me after my treatment was finished. "Today is your day to ring the bell," she said.

My face lit up. "I get to ring the bell?" I asked.

She said, "Yes, this was your last treatment."

I remember being exhausted that day, but hearing that gave me inner strength. I was going to ring the bell! I walked up to the bell in the hall, and before ringing it, I wished that I would never have to come back for treatment ever again. And I thanked God for sending my mother to me that night at the window and in my dreams, and for every day of my life.

Coming back into the waiting room after ringing the bell, I walked toward the locker room. People smiled and congratulated me. I said, "Thank you," and walked into the room to change, smiling too. I realized while changing that those were smiles of sincerity. Tears flooded my eyes because I knew there were people worse off than me that may never make it to ring the bell. My memory of their smiles lives with me every day and will for the rest of my life. God bless them all.

11

Rehabilitation Time

After all my treatments were finished, I found myself wanting to stay up late, sometimes to three or four o'clock in the morning. I felt time was valuable and being wasted. I didn't want to sleep. I relished every minute of my life and wanted to use my time awake rather than wasting it by sleeping. Maybe I felt that way because I felt so tired and slept a lot during the last three weeks of my treatments. I just wanted to stay awake as long as I could. Of course, I ended up going to bed after I couldn't keep my eyes open any longer, but then I woke up after what seemed like a short sleep to get on with my day.

One day, my husband suggested that I go up north to the cottage for a week or so by myself, along with our golden retriever, Buddy, to gather my thoughts, relax, and rehabilitate. So after thinking about it, I agreed. I packed up some of my things and Buddy's favorite toys, and away we went to the place that always gave me an inner peace and calm. We went for walks every day. I love to cook and made a lot of my favorite dishes. And depending on what it was and if not too spicy, I shared some with Bud. I loved that dog. I adopted him from a woman I used to work with. It was her son's dog, and he was moving and couldn't take Bud with him. He was three years old when we took him for ours. Our previous dog had just passed away at the age of thirteen, and I was lonely for a dog since I had dogs all my life. I almost didn't take Buddy. After telling my husband about Buddy and what kind of dog he was, my husband said he was too big. Compared to our beagle, Jingles, that just passed, I guess he was. He was a lot bigger, a little over a hundred pounds big, but when she brought in a picture and was going to hang it at work for a taker, I looked at that picture and fell in love with him. I said, "Oh, no. Don't hang it! I'll take him." My husband didn't know until he got home from work that night that I had brought Buddy to his new home. I introduced him. When my husband sat down on the sofa, Buddy went over to him and rested his head on his knee. That did it! Buddy won, and they became good friends.

I started to relax more and more each day at the cottage. After a nice walk, Buddy and I sat on the swing in the backyard, looking out over the water and the tall grasses swaying this way and that in the breeze. Buddy loved it there. Feeling not guilty, I actually started to take an afternoon nap every now and then. I could feel my mother near at times, but I didn't have any dreams with taps on the windows, and she didn't appear to me while I was there.

12

I Can Breathe Again

After all the walks and sitting in the backyard, I wanted to do something else and decided to draw. I had my drawing chalk there, but I needed a drawing tablet. So off to town I went and purchased one. I ended up drawing an eleven by fourteen picture of an owl. I had it framed, and it now hangs in our living room at home.

My husband came up every few days to see how I was doing. It was funny! It reminded me of our dating. So one time when he came up, I got silly and acted it out. I met him at the door and said, "Hello, Jim. It's so nice of you to stop by and visit. Come on in!" We laughed a lot, and it even got interesting. Then, after a cozy night stay, he'd leave for back home to work, and Buddy and I stayed and did an abundance of things.

I'm so glad my husband suggested I go up north and spend time at the cottage. It was the best therapy for me. I was paying attention to all the smaller things around me now as well as so much more. And I realized so much beauty God put on this earth for all of us. It's sad to take so much for granted when all the beauty and good can be taken away from us in a blink of an eye. There's so much to be thankful for. My values are different now. You really learn to respect your body. Listen to what it tells you. Most of all, don't ignore it. You only have one body; there's only one you.

It was such a blessed time at the cottage, but after spending a tranquil month there, I felt rejuvenated and missed home. It was time to go home.

13

Push Forward

Experiencing cancer is a traumatic experience for anyone. Each person handles it differently mentally and physically. Some can talk about it, and some people can't until they are ready. Some never talk about it. I'm one of those, "Can't until they are ready," people. It took me some years to really talk about it. The people there for you in this time of need are the greatest people in the world. They give you strength and hope to travel down the healing path. There is no room for negativity.

I believe knowledge is a recovery tool. Don't be afraid to ask your doctor questions. Ask about the new vaccines they offer and new cancer gene testing. Some clinics and hospitals offer free mammograms. Get the answers you are looking for. It helps so much to see the light on issues that allows you to accept them more and reduces your fears.

Prayers are always strong tools. I have two powerful ones that I still say. I have included them at the end of the book. I found they added comfort and helped me tremendously. I hope you find the same comfort with them as I did.

Everybody's life is different. Nothing is absolutely perfect, but we know to make the best of it and move on. So whatever negativity is in your life right now, keep pushing forward. Once you plow through, it's okay to look back because you know it's behind you now. Some things aren't easy to make go away, but stay strong, and don't give up. Have faith in yourself because you can do it. Just keep telling yourself, I can get through this," and you will.

14

Keeping Busy

My life is back to normal now, just like I wished for. I am so thankful. I have some side effects, but nothing I can't live with. I'm not complaining, believe me. My husband and I still walk a mile every morning up north at the cottage. Sometimes two. I continue my routine when I'm home.

I don't have my fun job at the craft store anymore. I think about going back, but I have so many other things right now keeping me busy. Canning is one. I love to cook and love gardening. I can about fifty quarts of tomatoes at the end of every summer. That's a lot, I know, but I like to give some away to friends and relatives. I love tomatoes, as you can tell, and make some of the best chili in the winter with them. Tomatoes are packed with vitamins—such as A, C, and E—and even some fiber; all are enemies of cancer-friendly free radicals. They are also low in fat and sodium, and rich in potassium. For people who don't like tomatoes or can't eat them for health reasons, there are many other fruits and vegetables that offer the same benefits.

Eating tomatoes has great benefits for men too. Eating them several times a week helps prevent prostate cancer. In its early stages, prostate cancer has no symptoms. It's often slow growing, and as it gets larger, it may cause problems with urination or create pain in the back, hip, thighs, or pelvis. The prostate-specific antigen (PSA) and (DRE) tests can detect prostate cancer. Men, like women, can get breast cancer, as well.

15

Gratefulness

I often feel my mother close, and I thank her every day. She gave me life when I was born, and she saved my life from being taken away. My mother was a beautiful, warm, loving, compassionate, and strong person. She was also a devoted Catholic. My mother was born in Rice, Minnesota, the middle child of five, and lived on a farm there. She moved to Michigan at a young age with her family and made it her home. She told me stories about her growing up, and I loved listening to them. She had a lot of struggles in her life but managed to jump those hurdles. She was my best friend and confidante. I know she is an angel, and God gave her wings to come to me that night at the window and in my dreams. I haven't had more dreams or her appearing in spirt form. Her job has been completed, and she successfully accomplished her mission. I wonder if she will have other assignments and what they would be. All I know is that whatever it is, she won't have a hard time getting anyone's attention. With every beat of my heart, I love you, Mom. A mother's love is forever.

Every year that goes by cancer-free, I am so grateful and feel blessed. I have an upcoming appointment with my oncologist in March 2017 for a CT scan and X-ray; I return April 5, 2017, for my results. If I get a good report, it will be nine and a half years cancer-free. They say if you reach ten years without recurrence, chances of it coming back are slim to none. I'm all for that and hope the same for all cancer patients and survivors.

I met with my oncologist on April 5, 2017, and my tests results from the CT scan and X-ray done in March came back good, and I was given a thumbs-up from my doctor. The doctor said it is unlikely my cancer will come back. My official date for my ten years cancer-free is December 19, 2017. It's September now, and I have three months to go until it's finally official. That day, leaving my doctor at the cancer institute, I thought of the bell on the wall I rang on the last day of my radiation treatment. I can't wait to ring the bell again on December 19 even louder with admiration for my mother and with forever thankfulness and love in my heart. It won't be the same bell, but ringing it will be felt, and I will hear it in my soul.

I wrote this book about my experience with cancer to help people understand they are not alone and that everybody's experience is unique. Time heals all wounds mentally and physically. Stay positive, and believe in your inner strength. It's there, and when you need it the most, it will surely surprise you.

Here are the two powerful prayers I would like to share with you.

THE MIRACLE PRAYER

Lord Jesus, I come before you just as I am. I am sorry for my sins. I repent of my sins. Please forgive me. In your name, I forgive all others for what they have done against me. I renounce Satan, the evil spirits, and all their works. I give you my entire self, Lord Jesus, now and forever. I invite you into my life, Jesus. I accept you as my Lord, God, and Savior. Please heal me, change me, and strengthen me in body, soul, and spirit.

Come, Lord Jesus, cover me with your precious blood, and fill me with your Holy Spirit. I love you, Lord Jesus. I praise you, Jesus. I thank you, Jesus. I shall follow you every day of my life. Amen.

Mary, my mother, Queen of Peace, St. Peregrine, the cancer saint, all you angels and saints, please help me.

Amen.

Say this prayer faithfully, no matter how you feel. When you come to the point where you sincerely mean each word with all your heart, something good spiritually will happen to you. You will experience Jesus, and he will change your whole life in a very special way. You will see.

1993 Servite Fathers, O.S.M.

PRAYER TO SAINT JOSEPH

O Saint Joseph, whose protection is so great, so strong, and so prompt before the Throne of God, I place in you all my interests and my desires.

O Saint Joseph, do assist me by your powerful intercession. Obtain for me from your Divine Son all spiritual blessings through Jesus Christ, our Lord, so that having benefited from your heavenly power, I may offer my thanksgiving and homage to the most loving of fathers.

O Saint Joseph, I never weary contemplating you and the Child Jesus asleep in your arms.

I dare not approach while he reposes near your heart.

Please press him in my name, and kiss his infant head for me.

And ask him to return the "kiss" when I draw my dying breath.

Saint Joseph, patron of departing souls, pray for us; pray for me.

Amen.

This is an extremely powerful prayer.

God listens, so talk to him even if it has been a long time since you attended Mass or said a prayer. He will listen.

CPSIA information can be obtained
at www.ICGtesting.com
Printed in the USA
LVOW11*2248110318
569415LV00002BA/3/P

9 781504 396042